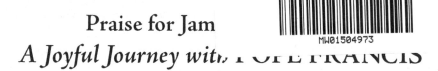

Praise for Jam
A Joyful Journey with POPE FRANCIS

"These succinct popularizations introduce us to the engaging vision of Pope Francis in summary form.... Hopefully, as you peruse these materials, you will discover that they are 'appetizers' for the full writings of Pope Francis. May you also discover the vibrant 'missionary spirit' of Pope Francis: 'Let us be realists, without losing our joy, our boldness, and our hope-filled commitment.'"

—CARDINAL LUIS ANTONIO TAGLE, PRO-PREFECT:
VATICAN DICASTERY OF EVANGELIZATION

✦ ✦ ✦

"James Kroeger provides a wonderful avenue for 'Catholics in the pews' (and others) to access the inspiring thought and vision of Pope Francis. In his synthesis of twelve major documents, Kroeger has faithfully captured the main points and phrases in this shortened and accessible format. We thank him for opening up the treasures of Pope Francis for a broader audience."

—ROGER SCHROEDER, SVD, CATHOLIC
THEOLOGICAL UNION, CHICAGO

✦ ✦ ✦

"James Kroeger has compiled a treasure trove of deeply meaningful and timely reflections on twelve writings from Pope Francis. These prophetic documents speak to important issues of our day and challenge us to respond with love and action."

—DIANE LAMPITT, M.ED., SPIRITUAL DIRECTOR,
CREATINGSOULSPACE.ORG

"A dozen pearls of wisdom for a dozen years of papal ministry! As Pope Francis compassionately continues guiding the People of God, this book recaps a dozen of his significant documents—an ideal way to again touch into his gifted wisdom and devoted fidelity. We have been privileged to be the recipients of a wealth of guidance—comfort and challenge—in Pope Francis' many and diverse writings. What a treasure this short compilation is—giving us reminders, recaps, summaries, and digests—when we might not have the time to delve deeply into each document. With its Reflection Questions and Prayer Prompts, this book is ideal for personal prayer and reflection, small faith-sharing groups, retreats, and parish adult faith formation."

—JANET SCHAEFFLER, OP, RETREAT/WORKSHOP
PRESENTER; AUTHOR

✦ ✦ ✦

"Before starting a road trip, especially one of any substance or length, we usually consult a map to get a bird's eye view of the starting point, destination, and points of interest along the way. Thus prepared, we travel with more confidence, anticipation, and orientation to our journey's end.

In *A Joyful Journey with Pope Francis*, Fr. Kroeger has given us road maps for twelve of Francis' most essential writings. These chapters are worthy and helpful companions for anyone who wants to engage with these groundbreaking exhortations and letters. If you have already read *Laudato Si* or *Amoris Laetitia*, these will help you organize and retain their teaching. If not, they will whet your appetite and encourage you to begin."

—TOM GOOD, PASTORAL MUSICIAN AND RESIDENT OFFICER,
NATIONAL LABOR RELATION BOARD (RETIRED)

"*A Joyful Journey with Pope Francis* packs an abundance of wisdom, insight, and powerful quotes from Pope Francis. It brilliantly synthesizes the Pope's deep and expansive thinking, as it clearly articulates the radical nature of the message of Christ and Francis' pontificate. A big treasure in a small package."

—GERARD THOMAS STRAUB, AUTHOR OF *READING THOMAS MERTON AND LONGING FOR GOD IN HAITI* (GERARDSTRAUB.COM)

✦ ✦ ✦

"Twelve years ago, Jorge Mario Bergoglio, a largely unknown Jesuit and Argentinian archbishop became Pope Francis, the 266th pope in the Catholic Church. Francis immediately became known for his humility, compassion, simplicity of lifestyle, and concern for the environment, just like his namesake, Francis of Assisi, the mystical saint known for joy, love, and passion for creation. Pope Francis has already left a legacy of inspiring documents that articulate his unique vision of the critically needed gifts the Catholic tradition offers to this challenging moment of the 21st century.

Fr. James Kroeger, MM, has summarized in a clear and concise manner the twelve key documents of Francis pontificate, making these foundational insights that will shape Catholicism for decades easily accessible to anyone. Here is a great chance to wade more deeply into the heart and mind of the mystical pope who has energized the Church and challenged it to think of itself not as a museum of religious ideas, perspectives, and images, but a "field hospital" that is prepared to serve the world by alleviating suffering and bringing a Gospel Joy to a troubled human condition.

—MARK S. MARKULY, PH.D., DEAN EMERITUS OF THE SCHOOL OF THEOLOGY AND MINISTRY, SEATTLE UNIVERSITY

A Joyful Journey with
POPE FRANCIS

EXPLORING TWELVE PIVOTAL DOCUMENTS

James H. Kroeger, MM

Faith Alive Books

Published by:

Faith Alive Books

GRAND RAPIDS, MICHIGAN
faithalivebooks.com

Copyright © 2024 by James H. Kroeger, MM

ISBN-13: 978-0-9998944-2-2

The original documents on which these summaries
are based can be found at www.vatican.va

Queries regarding rights and permissions should be addressed
to publisher Dan Pierson at danpierson@faithalivebooks.com

Subjects: Catholic Church—Doctrines. | Christian Ministry
| Christian Pastoral Resources | Francis, Pope, 1936–
Classification: BX1751.3 K76 2024 (print)

Cover and interior
Gary A. Rosenberg ✦ www.thebookcouple.com

Cover Photo
35294647 © Neneo | Dreamstime.com

Printed in the United States of America

Contents

Introduction

Popes have many titles, some classical, others popular. Of the classical appellations, Pope Francis would probably prefer "Servant of the servants of God." From the wide range of popular titles, he might choose "pope of mercy." He has incorporated this virtue into his papal motto: *miserando atque eligendo*, chosen through mercy. One constantly witnesses mercy through Francis' many actions and documents. In fact, he has asserted that Jesus is "mercy made flesh," born of the "Mother of Mercy" (MV 24).

Our merciful pope is now entering his twelfth year of guiding the People of God, having been elected on March 13, 2013. Recalling this milestone, this short booklet presents brief glimpses into twelve pivotal documents of the Francis pontificate. This writer is profoundly aware that no summaries can substitute for the rich depths of the full documents; these presentations are no more than enticements, appetizers, or inducements to savor Francis' profound wisdom and insights.

A quick glance at the table of contents will reveal the twelve documents found in this booklet; they are listed along with the descriptive title of each of the twelve chapters. Readers will note that the numbers found in parentheses after a quoted section in the text refer to the paragraphs of the original documents written by Pope Francis; these references will enable an interested person to easily locate the original text.

It is the sincere desire of this author that readers will see these materials as a kind of "road-map" to find and explore the rich treasures found in the corpus of Pope Francis' writings. Hopefully, it will prove to be a "joyful journey," an "enriching discovery," and a "rewarding pilgrimage"! Kindly note that at the end of each chapter there are "reflection questions" for personal or group use as well as a "prayer prompt" to initiate individual or shared prayer and commitment.

Finally, everyone will find Pope Francis to be a master teacher and a trustworthy guide, leading to a deeper "Christ-encounter." Let us often recall Francis' heartfelt exhortation: "I invite all Christians, everywhere, at this very moment, to a renewed personal encounter with Jesus Christ, or at least an openness to letting him encounter them; I ask all of you to do this unfailingly each day" (EG 3).

CHAPTER 1

Walking in the Light of Faith

*L*umen Fidei (LF), *The Light of Faith*, is Pope Francis' first encyclical. Francis admits that Pope Benedict XVI "had almost completed a first draft of an encyclical on faith" and for this initial work "I am deeply grateful to him." Here we have a unique treasure: profound reflections on faith from two popes!

As one reads, it becomes clear that Pope Benedict had the major input into this document. It harmonizes well with the vision Pope Benedict outlined in his proclamation of 2012 as a "year of faith," recalling the fiftieth anniversary of the opening of the Second Vatican Council (1962-1965).

Brief Overview

The structure of *Lumen Fidei* is simple and direct, containing an introduction and four chapters; it concludes with Marian reflections. The Introduction shows how ancients viewed faith; it narrates how the Second Vatican Council, a "Council on faith" sought to bring faith into the contemporary world. Francis writes: "The Second Vatican Council enabled the light of faith to illumine our human experience from within, accompanying the men and women of our time on their journey" (6).

Faith Foundations

Chapter One shows that we believe in a God of mercy and how Christians can "see with the eyes of Jesus and share in his mind" (21). "Faith opens the way before us and accompanies our steps through time. Hence, if we want to understand what faith is, we need to follow the route it has taken, the path trodden by believers" (8). "Believing means entrusting oneself to a merciful love which always accepts and pardons" (13).

In Chapter Two Francis portrays the close link between faith and truth. He asserts: "Faith transforms the whole person precisely to the extent that he or she becomes open to love" (26). "Christian faith, inasmuch as it proclaims the truth of God's total love and opens us to the power of that love, penetrates to the core of our human experience" (32).

Contemporary Faith

The importance of evangelization and the transmission of faith are central themes of Chapter Three. The communication of the gift of faith must be fostered in every age. "It is through an unbroken chain of witnesses that we come to see the face of Jesus" (38). Indeed, "the Church, like every family, passes on to her children the whole store of her memories" (40). For Francis, "the sacramental character of faith finds its highest expression in the Eucharist" (44).

Finally, in Chapter Four, Francis explains the link between faith and the common good. The Pope writes: "Precisely because it is linked to love (cf. Gal 5:6), the light of faith is concretely placed at the service of justice, law, and peace" (51). Faith enables us to share the gaze of Jesus and thus accompany the poor and suffering in our world.

Living the Faith

Pope Francis concludes his encyclical with some inspiring reflections on Mary's pilgrimage of faith (cf. 60). He prays: "Mother, help our faith! . . . Help us to entrust ourselves fully to him [Jesus] and to believe in his love, especially at times of trial, beneath the shadow of the cross, when our faith is called to mature."

The entire encyclical strikes a positive note as it unfolds how people through the centuries have lived their faith (e.g. Abraham, Moses, Saint Paul, Francis of Assisi, Mother Teresa of Calcutta, and the Virgin Mary). Faith, indeed, is a special gift that we pray may be granted to us, making us living icons of faith to others in the contemporary world.

➤ REFLECTION QUESTIONS

Who has been a powerful "faith witness" in your life? How did this person concretely manifest his/her faith; give some specific examples.

➤ PRAYER PROMPT

Lord, help me to be a true "faith witness" by . . .

CHAPTER 2

Living in Gospel Joy

Evangelii Gaudium (EG), *The Joy of the* Gospel [2013], Pope Francis' first apostolic exhortation, is lengthy, reaching over 50,000 words. Here Francis is proposing a profound missionary renewal of the entire Church, desiring a truly vibrant, evangelizing community, aflame with the fire of the Holy Spirit.

Francis says: "I dream of a 'missionary option,' that is, a missionary impulse capable of transforming everything" (27). He asserts: "All renewal in the Church must have mission as its goal if it is not to fall prey to a kind of ecclesial introversion" (27). He believes: "Missionary outreach is *paradigmatic for all the Church's activity*" (15).

Pope Francis' Vision

One may validly assert that this document summarizes the pope's theology, spirituality, and vision of pastoral-missionary ministry. His desire that the Church be "permanently in a state of mission" (25) comes from his deep personal relationship with Christ and he invites "all Christians, everywhere, at this very moment, to a renewed personal encounter with Jesus Christ" (3).

A pivotal insight of Francis is that "we are all missionary disciples" (119); "we no longer say that we are 'disciples' and 'missionaries,' but rather that we are always 'missionary disciples'" (120). "Missionary disciples accompany missionary disciples" (173). Evangelizers' lives must "glow with fervor" since they have received "the joy of Christ" (10).

Attracting Others

Pope Francis reveals a sense of humor at several points. He notes that unfortunately, "there are Christians whose lives seem like Lent without Easter" (6). "An evangelizer must never look like someone who has just come back from a funeral" (10). We must *not* become "querulous and disillusioned pessimists, 'sourpusses'" (85).

In EG Pope Francis makes following Jesus as his disciple an attractive invitation; this holds true because "being a Christian is not the result of an ethical choice or a lofty idea, but the encounter with an event, a person, which gives life a new horizon and a decisive direction" (8); cf. Benedict XVI.

Francis recognizes numerous mission challenges; yet, he remains realistically optimistic, asserting: "Challenges exist to be overcome! Let us be realists, but without losing our joy, our boldness and our hope-filled commitment. Let us not allow ourselves to be robbed of missionary vigor" (109)!

Ten Missionary Signposts

Evangelii Gaudium overflows with profound wisdom for Christian living and witness; this author now identifies pivotal, thematic insights which will contribute to renewing the missionary fervor of the Church.

1. *Missionaries as Christ-centered Persons.* Mission demands a "personal encounter with the saving love of Jesus." . . . The primary reason for evangelizing is the love of Jesus which we have received, the experience of salvation which urges us to ever greater love of him" (264).

2. *Joy as Pivotal Sign of Missionary Disciples.* Joyful evangelizers will contribute to a successful propagation of the Gospel. With heartfelt emotion, Pope Francis writes: "I wish to encourage the Christian faithful to embark upon a new chapter of evangelization marked by this joy" (1).

3. *Integrating Vatican II Perspectives.* Francis asserts that "it is important to draw out the pastoral consequences of the Council's teaching" (38) for worldwide mission today.

4. *Centrality of Mission in Church Life.* Francis constantly promotes an active missionary Church; as noted earlier, he proclaims that "missionary outreach is *paradigmatic for all the Church's activity*" (15).

5. *A Dynamic, Outgoing Church.* "I prefer a Church which is bruised, hurting and dirty because it has been out on the streets, rather than a Church which is unhealthy from being confined and from clinging to its own security" (49).

Additional Signposts

6. *Mercy is Central.* "The Church must be a place of mercy freely given, where everyone can feel welcomed, loved, forgiven, and encouraged to live the good life of the Gospel" (114).

7. *Social Involvement in Evangelization.* "Our faith in Christ, who became poor . . . is the basis of our concern for the integral development of society's most neglected members" (186).

8. *Popular Piety, a Vehicle of Evangelization.* "Popular piety enables us to see how the faith, once received, becomes embodied in a culture and is constantly passed on" (123).

9. *Dialogue in Evangelization.* Within a larger section on dialogue, Francis treats both ecumenical dialogue (244-249) and interreligious dialogue (250-254).

10. *World-wide Vision.* Undoubtedly, Pope Francis exhibits a broad vision of an evangelizing, collegial, and synodal Church, citing insights from numerous episcopal conferences from all across the world.

Sincere Invitation

Francis has issued a call for a missionary renewal of our Church; he is echoing the Second Vatican Council, which asserted that "the pilgrim Church is missionary by her very nature" (*Ad Gentes* 2). Let us joyfully heed Francis' heartfelt, personal invitation to become truly alive in mission!

➤ REFLECTION QUESTIONS

How do you see yourself as a "missionary disciple" in your present context? What factors could rob us of our missionary vigor?

➤ PRAYER PROMPT

Jesus, I want to be your "missionary disciple" through my . . .

CHAPTER 3

Proclaiming God's Boundless Mercy

A vast amount of "mercy material" from Pope Francis is available; however, probably the best source is Francis' 2015 document, *Misericordiae Vultus* [MV] (*The Face of Mercy*), wherein he proclaimed an entire *year of mercy* (2015–2016) to commemorate the fiftieth anniversary of the close of Vatican Council II (1965).

Summons to Compassion

Francis, the "Pope of Mercy," says: "We need constantly to contemplate the mystery of mercy. It is a wellspring of joy, serenity, and peace. . . . Mercy [is] the bridge that connects God and man" (2). Francis calls Christians to a renewed practice of the corporal and spiritual works of mercy (cf. 15). "Let us enter more deeply into the heart of the Gospel where the poor have a special experience of God's mercy" (15).

Our daily "living-in-mercy" is a duty for every Christian; it is not optional. Mercy is challenging; it is not easy. The demands of mercy are often inconvenient and unpredictable; it impinges on our personal plans and schedules. We cannot calculate when mercy will be demanded of us.

God, Father of Mercy

Francis notes that when mercy is shown it brings deep joy to God's heart. Scripture clearly affirms that God is "the Father of mercies and the God of all consolation" (2 Cor 1:3). Our God is "rich in mercy" (Eph 2:4), *dives in misericordia*. One of Jesus' well-known parables is that of the "merciful father" (though often known as the parable of the prodigal son): Lk 15:11-32. The magnanimous father shows his overflowing love, mercy and compassion to *both* of his sons. The parable reveals the overflowing mercy and tenderness of the compassionate father.

Jesus, Face of the Father's Mercy

Francis has written: "Mercy finds its most noble and complete expression in the Incarnate Word. Jesus reveals the face of the Father who is rich in mercy." In Jesus of Nazareth, mercy has become living and visible. Jesus' entire life and "his person is nothing but love, a love given gratuitously. . . . The signs he works, especially in the face of sinners, the poor, the marginalized, the sick, and the suffering, are all meant to teach mercy. Everything in him speaks of mercy. Nothing in him is devoid of compassion" (8).

Jesus often "felt deep compassion" for the crowds (Mt 9:36). He is moved with merciful compassion when he sees needy people. His mercy overflows when he invites Matthew the tax collector to follow him; he looked at Matthew with merciful love and chose him: *miserando atque eligendo* [Francis' episcopal motto] (Mt 9:9). Jesus spoke many parables devoted to mercy: the lost sheep, the lost coin, and the father with two sons (Lk 15:4-7, 8-10, 11-32).

Church, Community of Mercy

"Mercy is the very foundation of the Church's life. All of her pastoral activity should be caught up in the tenderness she makes present to believers; nothing in her preaching and in her witness to the world can be lacking in mercy. The Church's very credibility is seen in how she shows merciful and compassionate love. . . . The Church lives an authentic life when she professes and proclaims mercy" (11). "The Church is commissioned to announce the mercy of God, the beating heart of the Gospel, which in its own way must penetrate the heart and mind of every person" (12).

Christians, Missionaries of God's Mercy

Pope Francis frequently emphasizes the theme of mercy, noting that God's merciful love "is witnessed to by many men and women of every age and condition." Francis asserts that God's mercy "is all the more necessary when we consider how many injustices, wars, and humanitarian crises still need resolution." Francis frequently reminds priests (and all of us): "For the love of Jesus Christ, *never tire of being merciful!* . . . Have mercy, great mercy!"

Mary, Mother of Mercy

Pope Francis notes in *Misericordiae Vultus*: "My thoughts now turn to the Mother of Mercy. . . . No one has penetrated the profound mystery of the incarnation like Mary. Her entire life was patterned after the presence of mercy made flesh. . . . She treasured divine mercy in her heart. . . . Her hymn of praise [Lk 1:46-55] was dedicated to the mercy of God. . . . At the foot of the cross, Mary, together with John, the disciple of love, witnessed the words of forgiveness spoken by Jesus. This supreme expression of mercy towards those who crucified him shows us the point to which the mercy of God can reach" (24).

Conclusion

Pope Francis' Prayer for the Jubilee of Mercy sums up his vision: "Lord Jesus Christ, you have taught us to be merciful like the heavenly Father. . . . You are the face of the invisible Father, the God who manifests his power above all by forgiveness and mercy. Let your Church be your visible face in the world."

➤ REFLECTION QUESTIONS

Can you name one or two Church saints who could be called a "saint of mercy"? Briefly narrate his/her life story. From your own life experience, describe someone you know who is a true model of mercy and compassion.

➤ PRAYER PROMPT

Dear Mary, "Mother of Mercy," I want to show mercy by . . .

CHAPTER 4

Treasuring Our Common Home

Pope Francis has written a lengthy encyclical focused solely on the environment: *Laudato Sí* (LS), *On Care for Our Common Home*. Boldly, Francis argues that the environment is in crisis; he issues an urgent call to action. He pointedly asks: "What kind of world do we want to leave to those who come after us, to children who are now growing up?" (160).

Recalling the beautiful canticle of Francis of Assisi, the pope notes that the earth, our sister, "now cries out to us because of the harm we have inflicted on her by our irresponsible use and abuse of the goods with which God has endowed her" (2). "I would like to enter into dialogue with all people about our common home" (3). Throughout the *six* numbered chapters of *Laudato Sí*, [summarized in six paragraphs below], Francis calls for "a global ecological *conversion*" asserting that "authentic human development has a moral character" (5) and that we need "an integral ecology" (11).

1. **What is Happening to Our Common Home?** Straightforwardly, Francis asserts: "The earth, our home, is beginning to look more and more like an immense pile of filth" (21). "These problems are closely linked to a throwaway culture" (22). We have "a very solid scientific consensus" that sees that the cause is "mainly as a result of human activity" (23). Some key issues are: water (27-31), loss of biodiversity (32-42), decline in the quality of human life (43-47), global inequality (48-52), and weak responses (53-59). Thus,

15

we need to take a "frank look at the facts to see that our common home is falling into serious disrepair" (61).

2. **Gospel of Creation.** Francis sees "the rich contribution which religions can make towards an integral ecology and the full development of humanity" (62). The pope provides some insights: "We are not God. The earth was here before us and it has been given to us . . . to ensure its fruitfulness for coming generations" (67). "The work of the Church seeks not only to remind everyone of the duty to care for nature, but at the same time she must above all protect humankind from self-destruction" (79). We see "the earth is essentially a shared inheritance" (93) and "everything is related" (92). We need a sense of "deep communion with the rest of nature" (91), adopting "the gaze of Jesus" (96-100).

3. **Human Roots of the Ecological Crisis.** Pope Francis believes that "a certain way of understanding human life and activity has gone awry, to the serious detriment of the world around us" (101). Thus, there is a need to examine "the dominant technocratic paradigm" as well as "the place of human beings and of human action in the world" (101). We "need to slow down and look at reality in a different way" (114). "When we fail to acknowledge as part of reality the worth of a poor person, a human embryo, a person with disabilities—it becomes difficult to hear the cry of nature itself; everything is connected" (117). "A technology severed from ethics will not easily be able to limit its own power" (136).

4. **Integral Ecology.** Francis suggests that we now "consider some elements of an *integral ecology*, one which clearly respects its human and social dimensions" (137). "We are faced not with two separate crises, one environmental and the other social, but rather with one complex crisis which is both social and environmental" (139). Ecology must influence all of daily life (147-155). "The principle of the common good immediately becomes, logically

and inevitably, a summons to solidarity and a preferential option for the poorest of our brothers and sisters" (158). "The notion of the common good also extends to future generations" (159) [inter-generational justice]. "We need to see that what is at stake is our own dignity" (160). *Integral ecology* is a foundational principle!

5. **Lines of Approach and Action.** Francis next seeks "to outline the major paths of dialogue which can help us escape the spiral of self-destruction which currently engulfs us" (163). "Interdependence obliges us to think of *one world with a common plan*" (164). "What is needed is a politics which is far-sighted and capable of a new, integral and inter-disciplinary approach to handling the different aspects of the crisis" (197). Religions must continue in dialogue with science (199-201).

6. **Ecological Education and Spirituality.** "A great cultural, spiritual and educational challenge stands before us, and it will demand that we set out on the long path of renewal" (202). It must address "a consumerist lifestyle" (204). An "ecological conversion" is essential (216-221). Pope Francis believes there is hope, while admitting that his reflection is "both joyful and troubling" (246). Francis asks each of us to join him in promoting an "integral ecology."

➤ REFLECTION QUESTIONS

What are your personal, concrete initiatives to foster ecological responsibility? How can one's faith contribute to care for the earth, our common home?

➤ PRAYER PROMPT

St. Francis of Assisi, I promise to care for our "common home" by . . .

CHAPTER 5

Spreading the Joy of Love

Pope Francis has given an extraordinary gift to the Church: *Amoris Laetitia* (AL), *The Joy of Love*. This document focuses on the family and love. Francis draws heavily on the 2014 and 2015 world-wide Bishops' Synods on the Family; he enriches the discussion with his own pastoral insights.

Exploring the Treasures of *Amoris Laetitia*

Pope Francis himself provides an overview of the document. Various chapters examine (1) Scripture, (2) situation of families today, (3) Church teaching on marriage and the family, (4) love in marriage, (5) fruitful love, (6) pastoral approaches, (7) education of children, (8) Jesus' demands, and (9) family spirituality. Each chapter is a treasure-house of deep insight and wisdom!

Merciful Pastoral Tone

Pope Francis' letter sets an important pastoral agenda for the entire Church. He does not change any Church teaching, but he expresses his pastoral wisdom by always emphasizing mercy and compassion. He says: "I sincerely believe that Jesus wants a Church attentive to the goodness which the Holy Spirit sows in the midst of human weakness, a Mother who, while expressing her objective teaching, 'always does what good she can, even if in the process, her shoes get soiled by the mud of the street'" (308). In all situations, "the Church is commissioned to proclaim the mercy of God, the beating heart of the Gospel" (309).

Biblical Perspectives

The first chapter of *The Joy of Love* begins with a meditation on Psalm 128, a reading frequently chosen for both Jewish and Christian wedding liturgies: "Your wife will be like a fruitful vine within your house; your children will be like olive shoots around your table. . . . May you see your children's children"! The family is "the place where children are brought up in the faith" (16). "Every family should look to the icon of the Holy Family of Nazareth" (30).

Jesus and Families

"The Bible is full of families, births, love stories, and family crises" (8). In fact, "Jesus himself was born into a modest family"; [he] "visits the home of Peter, whose mother-in-law was ill. . . . He goes to the homes of tax collectors like Matthew and Zacchaeus . . . and speaks to sinners like the woman in the house of Simon the Pharisee. . . . He is also sensitive to the embarrassment caused by the lack of wine at a wedding feast" (21).

Challenges to Families Today

Pope Francis explores the current situation of families. He focuses on "concrete realities" in order to improve the Church's pastoral response, because he believes "the welfare of the family is decisive for the future of the world and that of the Church" (31). Families face many challenges; some examples are: migration, the "throw-away" culture, the anti-birth mentality, lack of housing and employment, pornography, the abuse of minors (cf. 39-56). Francis always asks the Church to "offer a word of truth and hope" (57).

Facing Actual Situations

The Church does well "to focus on concrete realities, since 'the call and the demands of the Spirit resound in the events of history'" (31). Migration needs to be faced because of "its negative effects on family life" (46). Some families may have a member who requires special care. Francis notes: "Families who lovingly accept the difficult trial of a child with special needs are greatly to be admired" (47). The Church seeks to help "families living in dire poverty and great limitations" (49).

Family Ministry Approaches

After reviewing the many contemporary challenges to family life, Pope Francis recommends a re-thinking of the approaches of the Church relative to marriage and family life. For Francis, it is not enough to stress "doctrinal, bioethical, and moral issues"; the Church must encourage "openness to grace" and "present marriage as a dynamic path to personal development and fulfillment.... We have been called to form consciences, not to replace them" (37).

Family: Sanctuary of Life

In a strongly worded section, Pope Francis presents his convictions about the sanctity of human life. "Here I feel it urgent to state that, if the family is the sanctuary of life, the place where life is conceived and cared for, it is a horrendous contradiction when it becomes a place where life is rejected and destroyed. So great is the value of a human life, and so inalienable the right to life of an innocent child growing in the mother's womb, that no alleged right to one's own body can justify a decision to terminate that life, which is an end in itself and which can never be considered the 'property' of another human being. The family protects human life in all its stages, including its last" (83).

Conclusion

This presentation highlights only a few significant insights of *The Joy of Loving*, useful for your meditation, enrichment, and prayer. A reflective reading Pope Francis' original text will certainly prove wonderfully rewarding!

➤ REFLECTION QUESTIONS

What are some concrete instances in your family that manifested genuine love and faith? How, in specific ways, might we serve struggling families?

➤ PRAYER PROMPT

Lord, I promise to spread the true "joy of love" by . . .

CHAPTER 6

Rejoicing in Gladness – Always

Gaudete et Exsultate (GE) is the third Apostolic Exhortation issued by Pope Francis, following *Evangelii Gaudium* (2013) and *Amoris Laetitia* (2016). It is a call to holiness of life, clearly echoing the universal call to holiness found in Vatican II's *Lumen Gentium* chapter five; it is dated March 19, 2018, the feast of Saint Joseph, the fifth anniversary of his inauguration as pope in 2013.

Introduction

Gaudete et Exsultate (GE) is meant to be very practical; it is *not* intended to be a total synthesis of holiness or spirituality today. Its title emerges from scripture, specifically Matthew 5:12, where Jesus advises his disciples to "rejoice and be glad"—even in the midst of life's trials. Francis notes:"My modest goal is to re-propose the call to holiness in a practical way for our own time" (2). The Lord "wants us to be saints and not to settle for a bland and mediocre existence" (1).

The Call to Holiness

There are many forms of holiness, and in our holiness pilgrimage, "we are in the company of the great saints, martyrs, and witnesses who sustain us in our journey" (4). "We are all called to be witnesses, but there are many actual ways of bearing witness" (11). Francis praises what he calls "the middle class of holiness" (7); this includes parents, workers, sick/elderly, grandparents. Holiness is often found "in our next-door neighbors" (7). A simple norm is: "Each in his or her own way" (11). "For God's life is communicated to some in one way and to others in another" (11).

"This holiness to which the Lord calls you will grow through small gestures" (16). We "need only find a more perfect way of doing what we are already doing" (17). "A Christian cannot think of his or her mission on earth without seeing it as a path of holiness" (19). "You too need to see the entirety of your life as a mission" (23). "Life does not have a mission, but is a mission" (27). Francis quotes the words of Leon Bloy: "The only great tragedy in life is not to become a saint" (34).

Two Subtle Enemies of Holiness

Pope Francis mentions two false forms of holiness that "can lead us astray" (35): *gnosticism* (belief that salvation can be had through "special knowledge") and *pelagianism* (belief that we can attain salvation through our own human efforts) (35). He quotes Saint Bonaventure who pointed out that "true Christian wisdom can never be separated from mercy towards our neighbor" (46). We must constantly recall that "our life is essentially a gift" (55).

Following Jesus

The third chapter centers on the example of Jesus, specifically on the Beatitudes and Matthew 25:31-46 (Last Judgment narrative). "The Beatitudes are like a Christian's identity card" (63). Yes, we radically defend "the innocent unborn," but "equally sacred . . . are the lives of the poor, those already born, the destitute, the abandoned and the underprivileged, the vulnerable infirm and elderly exposed to covert euthanasia, the victims of human trafficking, new forms of slavery, and every form of rejection" (101). "Mercy is the very foundation of the Church's life" (105).

Five Signs of Holiness

First, there is **perseverance, patience** and **meekness.** Secondly, one needs **joy** and **a sense of humor,** because "ill humor is no sign of holiness" (126). Thirdly, **boldness** and **passion** are needed. "Holiness is *parrhesia;* it is boldness, an impulse to evangelize . . ." (129). "Boldness and apostolic courage are an essential part of mission" (131). "The Church needs passionate missionaries" (138).

Two additional manifestations of holiness are: **community** and **constant prayer.** "Growth in holiness is a journey in community, side by side with others" (141); it is "made up of small everyday things" (143). "Moments spent alone with God are also necessary; . . . this is true not only for a privileged few, but for all of us" (149). Francis notes the centrality of the Eucharist (157).

Spiritual Combat, Vigilance and Discernment.

"The Christian life is a constant battle. We need strength and courage to withstand the temptations of the devil and to proclaim the Gospel" (158). We have been given "powerful weapons" to assist us in our battle: "faith-filled prayer, meditation on the Word of God, the celebration of Mass, Eucharistic adoration, sacramental Reconciliation, works of charity, community life, missionary outreach" (162). Francis bluntly states that discernment "is a gift which we must implore" (166). Discernment is about "recognizing how we can better accomplish the mission" (174). "God asks everything of us, yet he also gives everything to us" (175).

Final Invocation

Francis invokes Mary, "the saint among the saints" (176). Thus, we must constantly turn to Mary, "because she lived the Beatitudes of Jesus as none other. . . . Our converse with her consoles, frees, and sanctifies us. . . . All we need do is whisper, time and time again: 'Hail Mary . . .'" (176).

➤ REFLECTION QUESTIONS

Who are some persons in your life who manifested "everyday holiness"? Why is "quiet time" necessary to make progress in holiness?

➤ PRAYER PROMPT

Jesus, assist me to integrate "everyday holiness" in my life by . . .

CHAPTER 7

Journeying with Today's Youth

Pope Francis marked the feast of the Annunciation in 2019 by releasing his apostolic exhortation *Christus Vivit* (CV), *Christ Lives*; it is the fruit of listening and discerning during the October 2018 Synod of Bishops, focused on the theme: "Young People, the Faith and Vocational Discernment."

Structure

The inviting document is presented in nine chapters, roughly corresponding to the pastoral method of "see, judge, act" or, in the framework of the Asian bishops, "dialogue, discernment, deeds." Succinctly presented, the first three chapters present "observations" (scriptural, theological, sociological); the middle three chapters offer an "assessment" (spiritual, developmental, generational); the final three chapters focus on "action" (pastoral, missionary, synodal). Taken together, *Christus Vivit* constitutes a *magna carta* for youth and pastoral ministry.

Christological Emphases

Several rich themes emerge from a comprehensive review of this lengthy document. There is a clear emphasis on Christ; Francis asserts: "Christ is alive! He is our hope, and in a wonderful way he brings youth to our world. The very first words, then, that I would like to say to every young Christian are these: Christ is alive and he wants you to be alive" (1).

Personal Relationship

"He [Christ] is in you; he is with you and he never abandons you. However far you may wander, he is always there, the Risen One. He calls you and he waits for you to return to him and start over again. When you feel you are growing old out of sorrow, resentment or fear, doubt or failure, he will always be there to restore your strength and your hope" (2). The Church should not be "excessively caught up in herself, but instead, and above all, reflect Jesus Christ" (39). "In Jesus, all the young [indeed everyone] can see themselves" (31).

Church: An Open Community

What vision of the Church emerges in *Christus Vivit?* Pope Francis explores the relationship between the young and the entire People of God, both pastors and faithful. There is not a separate "Church of the young" or a "Church with the young and for the young." There exists a single community, the Church—and the young are living and creative members of this one body.

Synodal Church

Pope Francis emphasizes the importance of synodality (walking together) in the Church. All segments of the Church (young, old, lay, ordained, religious, married, etc.) are to collaborate in building a better future. Francis also speaks on specific issues. For example, he invites the entire Church to reach out to migrants, following a balanced approach to this often-divisive issue. He also encourages young people through media to share the beauty of their own personal experience of encounter with Christ, an important avenue for building up Christ's Church.

Gospel Insights

Francis explores Scripture in this pastoral letter, written "with great affection" (3). He writes: "In the Gospel of Mathew, we find a young man (Mt 19:20-22) who approaches Jesus and asks if there is more that he can do; in this, he demonstrates that youthful openness of spirit which seeks new horizons and great challenges. Yet, his spirit was really not that young, for he had already become attached to riches and comforts. He said he wanted something more, but when Jesus asked him to be generous and distribute his goods, he realized that he could not let go of everything he had. . . . He had given up his youth" (18).

Matthew's Gospel (25:1-13) also "speaks about a group of wise young women, who were ready and waiting, while others were distracted and slumbering." The Pope notes: "We can, in fact, spend our youth being distracted, skimming the surface of life, half-asleep, incapable of cultivating meaningful relationships or experiencing the deeper things in life. In this way, we can store up a paltry and unsubstantial future. Or we can spend our youth aspiring to beautiful and great things, and thus store up a future full of life and interior richness" (19).

Concluding Reflections

Presented in a unique style expressive of closeness, frankness, simplicity, tenderness, and warmth, Pope Francis in *Christus Vivit* is eliciting our personal response. With pastoral boldness, Francis is inviting all in the Church to become a serving Church, one that is not silent or afraid to speak to pivotal issues facing the world today; this means fostering a humble community, one that listens, particularly to the insights of the youth.

Francis asks all to turn to Mary as "the supreme model for a youthful Church that seeks to follow Christ with enthusiasm and docility" (43). We can only meet these many challenges, if we personally "encounter each day your best friend, the friend who is Jesus" (151). Obviously, Pope Francis is speaking from his heart to our hearts, inviting us to strive to be "open-hearted" missionary-disciples!

➤ REFLECTION QUESTIONS

What are some of the main obstacles youth face in following Christ today? How can committed Christians assist in overcoming these challenges?

➤ PRAYER PROMPT

Jesus, help me to be a missionary to today's youth by . . .

CHAPTER 8

Discovering the Amazonian Church

ollowing the 2019 Bishops' Synod on the Pan-Amazon region, Pope Francis issued on February 2, 2020 his reflections in the form of an apostolic exhortation, *Querida Amazonia* (QA), *Beloved Amazon*. This is his fifth exhortation, coming after *Evangelii Gaudium* (2013), *Amoris Laetitia* (2016), *Gaudete et Exsultate* (2018), and *Christus Vivit* (2019). Originally written in Spanish, *Querida Amazonia* has been widely translated.

Beloved Amazon is of modest length (16,000 words) and divided into 111 sections in four chapters. Each chapter is focused on one of "four great dreams" that the Amazon region inspires in Francis; his dreams are social, cultural, ecological, and ecclesial. Since the renewed emphasis on synods emerging in the Vatican II era, this is the first to be centered on a distinct ecological territory. The Amazon region has about 34 million inhabitants, including three million indigenous people from nearly 400 ethnic groups; the territory covers nine various countries.

Four Dreams

Pope Francis himself provides a succinct overview of the document; he summarizes his *four dreams* in section seven of the introduction.

Social

"I dream of an Amazon region that fights for the rights of the poor, the original peoples and the least of our brothers and sisters, where their voices can be heard and their dignity advanced."

Cultural

"I dream of an Amazon region that can preserve its distinctive cultural riches, where the beauty of our humanity shines forth in so many varied ways."

The Pope continues highlighting his dreams:

Ecological

"I dream of an Amazon region that can jealously preserve its overwhelming natural beauty and the superabundant life teeming in its rivers and forests."

Ecclesial

"I dream of Christian communities capable of generous commitment, incarnate in the Amazon region, and giving the Church new faces with Amazonian features." Uniquely, these dreams are elaborated in a very artistic and literary manner, often employing original indigenous poetry.

Social Insights

Francis is deeply concerned about environmental and ecological stewardship, not only for Amazonia, but for the entire world; "the mission that God has entrusted to us all [is] the protection of our common home" (19). "Efforts to build a just society require a capacity for fraternity, a spirit of human fellowship" (20).

Social dialogue is needed worldwide. Francis asserts: "If we wish to dialogue, we should do this in the first place with the poor. . . . They are our principal partners, those from whom we have the most to learn. . . . Their words, their hopes, and their fears should be the most authoritative voice at any table of dialogue . . ." (26). Indeed, "a prophetic voice must be raised, and we as Christians are called to make it heard" (27).

Cultural Dreams

Pope Francis emphasizes a holistic cultural approach in the Church's mission, stating that there is an urgent need "to respect the rights of peoples and cultures" (40). He speaks very personally: "I urge the young people of the Amazon region . . . to take charge of your roots, because from the roots comes the strength that will make you grow, flourish, and bear fruit" (33). "Starting from our roots, let us sit around the common table, a place of conversation and shared hopes" (37). The Church's mission seeks to promote an authentic diversity, incorporating "dialogue between different cultural visions of celebration, of interrelationship, and of revival of hope" (38).

Ecological Perspectives

As Christians we have an obligation "to care for our brothers and sisters and the environment" because "alongside the ecology of nature there exists what can be called a 'human' ecology which in turn demands a 'social' ecology" (41). "To abuse nature is to abuse our ancestors, our brothers and sisters, creation and the Creator, and to mortgage the future" (42).

Pope Francis believes that the indigenous peoples can teach us to practice the "prophecy of contemplation" (53), entering into communion with the mystery of nature; we can "love it, not simply use it" (55). We are summoned to avoid "a consumerist lifestyle" which leads to "violence and mutual destruction" (59). "Let us awaken our God-given aesthetic and contemplative sense" (56)!

Ecclesial Contributions

Francis repeatedly emphasizes the Church's task of inculturating the Gospel, because "a faith that does not become culture is a faith not fully accepted, not fully reflected upon, not faithfully lived" (67). In her mission, the Church must seek to capitalize on the popular religiosity of indigenous people (77-80). Francis believes that "popular piety can enable us to see how the faith, once received, becomes embodied in a culture and is constantly passed on" (78). This effort will result in "an inculturated spirituality" (79).

Additional Insights

In *Querida Amazonia* one finds many deep insights on the Eucharist, women, holiness, and God's revelation through "two human faces: the face of his divine Son made man and the face of a creature, a woman, Mary" (101). Friends, discover and enjoy another "Francis treasure"!

➤ REFLECTION QUESTIONS

What specific insights can we learn from indigenous peoples, their cultures and spiritualities? What blinds us from appreciating their contributions?

➤ PRAYER PROMPT

Lord, I need your help to accept people of ethnic diversity, by . . .

CHAPTER 9

Fostering Fraternity and Friendship

On the eve of the October 4 feast of Saint Francis of Assisi in 2020, Pope Francis released his third encyclical entitled *Fratelli Tutti* (FT), *Brothers/Sisters All*. As with Francis' second encyclical, *Laudato Sí*, the Italian title is drawn from the writings of the pope's namesake, Francis of Assisi, who lived in the twelfth century and is now the patron saint of ecology.

Fratelli Tutti is lengthy (43,000 words); however, its sheer size should not eclipse its relevant and urgent message! A few of its key themes are the following: renewed human relationships on all levels of society, the call for peace and reconciliation, the renewal of politics, care for the earth our common home, more cordial relations between Christianity and Islam, and religions at the service of human solidarity. The individual chapters of *Fratelli Tutti* can serve as a walking tour of the encyclical.

Chapter One, "Dark Clouds over a Closed World," summarizes numerous challenges facing humanity today. Pope Francis notes that "as society becomes ever more globalized, it makes us neighbors, but does not make us brothers" (12). He also recalls that Francis of Assisi listened to God, the poor, the infirm, and nature; this seed planted by Francis needs to grow in our hearts (cf. 48).

Chapter Two, entitled "A Stranger on the Road," is a marvelous reflection on Jesus' Good Samaritan parable (Lk 19:25-37). The Pope observes that this parable shows us that true community can only be built by men and women who identify with the vulnerability of others (cf. 67). Francis notes that there are many "injured" people in our world; he asserts that we must actually touch them, not only sympathize with them at a safe distance (cf. 76).

Chapter Three, "Envisioning and Engendering an Open World," outlines a vision of human solidarity. Francis returns to the Good Samaritan parable; he observes that those who passed by the wounded man were concerned with their duties, their social status, and their professional commitments; the wounded man on the road-side was only a "distraction" from their personal, important daily duties (cf. 101). All people must grow in human awareness; we need "the spark of universal consciousness" (117).

Chapter Four asserts that everyone needs "A Heart Open to the Whole World." This means appreciating diverse peoples, cultures, religions, and values. It demands recognizing that all individuals are to be seen as gifts, bringing opportunities for enrichment and integral human development (cf. 133). Francis asserts: "We need to develop the awareness that nowadays we are all saved together or no one is saved" (137).

Three chapters summarize some urgent needs of humanity today: "A Better Kind of Politics" [5], "Dialogue and Friendship in Society" [6], and "Paths of Renewed Encounter" [7]. We can appreciate the multiple, insightful comments of Pope Francis. He notes that world politics must address hunger; discarded food constitutes a genuine scandal. "Hunger is criminal; food is an inalienable right" (189).

Authentic politics needs to make room for the tender love of others; tenderness is the path of choice for the most courageous men and women (cf. 194). Francis believes that "life, for all its confrontations, is the art of encounter" (215); thus, we seek to promote the growth of the "culture of encounter," seeking to transcend differences and divisions (cf. 215). It is important "to create *processes* of encounter, processes that build a people that can accept differences" (217).

Additional Insights

In *Fratelli Tutti* one finds numerous suggestions to facilitate authentic human encounter and thus foster community and solidarity. Genuine peace is only achieved through dialogue, reconciliation, and mutual development (cf. 229). As the Latin American bishops have noted: "The option for the poor should lead us to friendship with the poor" (234). We need to keep our historical memory alive, remembering such tragedies as the *Shoah*, the atomic bombs dropped on Hiroshima and Nagasaki, and the slave trade (cf. 247-248).

Chapter Eight, the final chapter, "Religions at the Service of Fraternity in Our World," portrays the pivotal contribution that the world's diverse religions can make to building fraternity and defending justice in the wider society.

Practical Applications

As we seek to grow in our faith and social commitment, we look for concrete paths to make progress; certainly, reading and absorbing the deep insights of Pope Francis' writings will profoundly enrich us. Consider *Fratelli Tutti* as a vast smorgasbord of fine food; taste and savor all its rich fare. One might read a chapter a week, devote fifteen minutes to reflective meditation daily, or bring the full encyclical on your annual retreat. Whatever your choice, commit to absorbing and implementing the vision and dreams of Pope Francis on fraternity and social friendship. Truly, you will discover that we are *"fratelli tutti,"* "brothers and sisters all"!

➤ REFLECTION QUESTIONS

Can you describe a situation when you encountered someone of a very different personality or culture and you became friends? What are some obstacles that prevent our growth in human and social solidarity?

➤ PRAYER PROMPT

Creator God, assist me listen to the "cry of our wounded earth" by . . .

CHAPTER 10

Continuing Our Liturgical Formation

Aprecious gift from Pope Franics is *Desiderio Desideravi* (DD), *On Liturgical Formation*; this apostolic letter calls for the rediscovery of the beauty of the liturgy and its central importance in the life of the Church. Issued on the feast of Saints Peter and Paul (June 29, 2022), this medium-length document is the pope's second document on the liturgy, following his 2021 *Traditionis Custodes* which sought to place limits on the use of the pre-Vatican II liturgy by groups opposed to the pivotal reforms of the Second Vatican Council (1962-1965).

Precious Resource

This present letter is a powerful teaching document and a text for meditation; it reveals the deep liturgical and spiritual insights of Pope Francis that emerge from his many decades of living and celebrating the Paschal Mystery. For Francis—and everyone—to participate "at Eucharist is to be plunged into the furnace of God's love" (57).

One may view the document as having the following three major topics or sections: liturgy in the life of the Church (2-26), the need for serious and vital liturgical formation (27-47), and *ars celebrandi*, the art of celebrating (48-60); there is also a brief introduction and conclusion. Pope Francis notes that he is writing this letter to share with all in the Church "some reflections on the liturgy, a dimension fundamental for the life of the Church" (1). The title, *Desiderio Desideravi*, is drawn from the words of Jesus in Luke 22:15, expressing his desire to eat the Passover with his disciples before he suffers.

Liturgical Foundations

Part One provides a scriptural basis, a theology of the liturgy, some current difficulties, and the challenge to "live" the liturgy in daily life. Francis notes that we all should consider ourselves as "privileged invitees" to the Lord's table; we, in turn, should not rest until the same invitation has been extended to all through the implementation of the Church's "missionary option," the fervent dream Pope Francis highlighted in *Evangelii Gaudium* (27).

Francis recalls that the Second Vatican Council and the liturgical movement promoted the rediscovery of the theological understanding of the liturgy and its importance in the life of the Church, promoting its "full, conscious, active, and fruitful celebration" (cf. SC 14). In the words of Saint Augustine, the Eucharist is "the sacrament of mercy, the sign of unity, and the bond of charity."

Conciliar Insights

The second part of the document beautifully presents the liturgical renewal of the Second Vatican Council and its foundational role in the Church's life; here Francis eloquently connects the acceptance of the renewed liturgy with the very acceptance of the Council itself. Thus, one understands the urgent need for a deep, ongoing liturgical formation for all members of the Church.

To appreciate the comprehensive renewal of Vatican II, one must read in harmony its four great constitutions: *Lumen Gentium*

(Church), *Dei Verbum* (Revelation), *Gaudium et Spes* (Church in the Modern World), and *Sacrosanctum Concilium* (Liturgy). In addition, recall that an ecumenical council is the highest expression of synodality in the Church—and Vatican II began its *aggiornamento* (renewal, updating) with reflection on the liturgy. Although six decades have passed since the Council began in 1962, its deep insights remain foundational for our Church.

Liturgical Celebration: An Art

Part Three on the art of celebrating presents numerous pivotal themes; some examples are: celebrating is an "art"; it requires "consistent application" and a deeper appreciation of symbols; all are to enter into the action of the Holy Spirit forming the Christian community at prayer; moments of silence are essential.

Pope Francis notes that when the early Christian community broke bread following the Lord's command, they did so under that gaze of Mary (Acts 1:14). As Mary protected the Word made flesh in her womb, she now protects those being formed in the womb of the Church that protects the Eucharist, the body of Christ (cf. 58).

Special Emphases

Another crucial topic emerges at various points in the document: full acceptance of the entire corpus of Church teaching found in the sixteen documents of Vatican II. Emphatically, Francis asserts that there can be no retreat "to that ritual form which the Council fathers, *cum Petro et sub Petro* [with Peter (as Pope) and under Peter] felt the need to reform, approving [the revised liturgy] under the guidance of the Holy Spirit and following their consciences as pastors" (61).

The pope also notes that an Ecumenical Council like Vatican II is a pivotal expression of the Church's synodality (cf. 29). Clearly, speaking from the heart, Francis asks us "to listen together to what the Spirit is saying to the Church. Let us safeguard our communion. Let us continue to be astonished at the beauty of the Liturgy. All this under the gaze of Mary, Mother of the Church" (65)!

➤ REFLECTION QUESTIONS

What are some specific ways that the Eucharist renews and transforms you? How can the Church better attract young people to the Eucharist?

➤ PRAYER PROMPT

Jesus, I hope to share my faith in your true Eucharistic presence by . . .

CHAPTER 11

Calling for Urgent Climate Action

I n October 2023, Pope Francis issued a passionate call "to all people of good will on the climate crisis." Releasing his apostolic exhortation *Laudate Deum* (LD), *Praise God* on October 4, the feast of Saint Francis of Assisi, the Pope enunciates a prophetic call to seriously address the contemporary environmental and ecological crises humanity is experiencing.

Present Context

This document arrives eight years after Pope Francis published his *Laudato Si*, which bore the subtitle "On Care for Our Common Home" [2015 / 2023]. Francis desires to share his "heartfelt concerns about the care of our common home" and "our suffering planet"; he feels a deep sense of urgency because "our responses have not been adequate" (2). Thus, in *Laudate Deum* Francis seeks to spark a serious examination of conscience with a concomitant commitment to decisive action!

Describing the Situation

Francis notes that "despite all attempts to deny, conceal, gloss over, or relativize the issue, the signs of climate change are here and increasingly evident" (5). Francis offers a realistic analysis; the evaluation is based on solid science and accurate statistics. It is no longer possible to doubt the "human origins" of climate change; unfortunately, some effects of the climate crisis are already irreversible.

Critiquing a Paradigm

In *Laudato Sí* the Pope presented the "technocratic paradigm" that underlies the current reality of environmental decay; this paradigm continues to advance. It is based on a false vision that idolizes technology and economic profit over human responsibility, values, and conscience. The human family needs "a sound ethics, a culture and spirituality genuinely capable of setting limits and teaching clear-minded self-restraint" (24).

Politics and Climate Conferences

These two areas are covered in sections three and four of *Laudate Deum*. Pope Francis readily admits that "goodness, together with love, justice and solidarity, are not achieved once and for all; they have to be realized each day" (34). Genuine progress requires "effective world organizations, equipped with the power to provide for the global common good, the elimination of hunger and poverty, and the sure defense of fundamental human rights" (35). Unfortunately, such effective cooperation is painfully slow in emerging!

Motives for Action

The final section of *Laudate Deum* presents "spiritual motivations" for commitment and engagement in climate action. Francis notes that Jesus himself was acutely sensitive before the creatures of his Father, speaking of the lilies of the field (Mt 6:28-29) and many sparrows (Lk 12:6). Truly, Jesus "was able to invite others to be attentive to the beauty that there is in the world because he himself was in constant touch with nature" (65).

Conclusion

It is noteworthy that Pope Francis begins and ends *Laudate Deum* with the imperative to "Praise God," to clearly recognize God's sovereignty and the divine in all of creation and the entire universe. Praise God! Only God! Always God!

➤ REFLECTION QUESTIONS

What concrete steps can be taken to raise people's awareness about the ecological crisis? How can one's faith influence this urgent challenge?

➤ PRAYER PROMPT

Loving God, I desire to begin healing "our suffering planet" by . . .

CHAPTER 12

Trusting in God's Merciful Love

Pope Francis, marking the 150th anniversary of Thérèse of Lisieux's birth (1873-2023), published an apostolic exhortation entitled *C'est la Confiance* (CC). It bears the subtitle: "On Confidence in the Merciful Love of God."

Introducing Thérèse

Pope Francis notes that Thérèse is "one of the best known and most loved saints in our world" (4). Thérèse interacted with several popes. Leo XIII allowed her at age 15 to enter the Carmelite convent. She died of tuberculosis on September 30, 1897 at the age of 24.

Only 28 years later in 1925, Pius XI canonized her and two years later made her patron saint of missions. In 1997, John Paul II declared her Doctor of the Church. Pope Francis canonized her parents, Louis and Zélie Martin, during the Synod on the Family in 2015. Her feast day is October 1.

A Profound Spirituality

Widespread interest in Thérèse was sparked by the posthumous publication of her autobiography, *The Story of a Soul*; it describes her unique insights into the spiritual life. It is the desire of Pope Francis that Thérèse's message may "be taken up as part of the spiritual treasury of the Church" (4). He also quotes Pope John Paul II who referred to Thérèse as "an expert in the *scientia amoris*" (science of love).

Pope Francis notes that "the final pages of her *Story of a Soul* are a missionary testament expressing her appreciation that evangelization takes place by attraction, not by pressure or proselytism" (10). Thérèse believed that when the soul is drawn to Jesus it "plunges into the shoreless ocean of your love" (10). Francis asserts that "this is what happened, especially after her death. It was her promised 'shower of roses'" (13).

Little Way of Trusting Love

Thérèse used the image of an elevator in her *Story of a Soul* to describe her "little way." "The elevator which must raise me to heaven is your arms, O Jesus! And for this, I had no need to grow up, but rather I had to remain *little* and become this more and more" (16). Francis affirms: "Little, incapable of being confident in herself, and yet firmly secure in the loving power of the Lord's arms" (16).

Thérèse was delirious with joy when she found her special vocation. "My vocation is Love. Yes, I have found my place in the Church. . . . In the heart of the Church, my Mother, I shall be *Love*. Thus, I shall be everything, and thus my dream will be realized" (39). "This was the radical option of Thérèse, her definite synthesis and her deepest spiritual identity" (41).

Francis' Concluding Prayer

"Dear Saint Thérèse, the Church needs to radiate the brightness, the fragrance and joy of the Gospel. Send us your roses! Help us to be, like yourself, ever confident in God's immense love for us, so that we may imitate each day your 'little way' of holiness. Amen." (53).

➤ REFLECTION QUESTIONS

Why are so many ordinary people deeply attracted to Thérèse's "little way"? What virtues can Thérèse teach us today in our contemporary society?

➤ PRAYER PROMPT

Dear St. Thérèse, I will help spread your loving roses by . . .

Concluding Synthesis

Our twelve-stop pilgrimage with Pope Francis has been an enriching experience. Several "Francis themes" have surfaced during our rewarding journey.

Implementing the Second Vatican Council

Clearly Pope Francis has sought to bring the Council's vision of renewal to the heart of the Church. Celebrating the feast of Saint John XXIII, convoker of Vatican II, Francis notes: "Let us return to the Council's pure sources of love. Let us rediscover the Council's passion and renew our own passion for the Council."

Becoming a Missionary People

Repeatedly Pope Francis calls the entire Church to a new chapter of evangelization, inviting every Christian to a life of missionary discipleship. As those who have encountered Jesus, we are to share the joy of the Gospel. Our mission as disciples of Christ Jesus "is at once a passion for Jesus and a passion for his people" (EG 268).

Caring for Our Common Home

Pope Francis is passionately concerned with environmental and ecological issues that profoundly affect the earth and all living beings.

He has written two pivotal documents on this topic: *Laudato Sí* (2015) and *Laudate Deum* (2023). Addressing climate change is undoubtedly a key pillar of his papacy.

Living Merciful Lives

Pope Francis, often called the "pope of mercy," proclaimed an entire *year of mercy* in his 2015 *Misericordiae Vultus*, commemorating the fiftieth anniversary of the close of Vatican II (1965-2015). Francis says: "We need constantly to contemplate the mystery of mercy. It is a wellspring of joy, serenity, and peace. . . . Mercy [is] the bridge that connects God and man" (MV 2).

Seeking Authentic Holiness

Francis consistently calls all to holiness in daily life; this summons clearly emerges in his 2018 apostolic exhortation *Gaudete et Exsultate*. We are to become saints, not simply settling for "a bland and mediocre existence" (GE 1). Francis asserts that the Beatitudes provide a pathway for holiness outlined by Jesus himself.

Experiencing Church as Community

Pope Francis encourages Catholics to be active members of the Church, despite its failures and imperfections, because the Church is a pivotal place where one can find Jesus.

Final Invitation

We all know that walking contributes to our physical health. You are invited to *take a long walk* with Pope Francis; it will prove beneficial for your spiritual well-being. In addition, you will discover that it is a joyful journey in faith!

About the Author

Father James H. Kroeger, a Maryknoll Missioner, has served mission in Asia (Philippines and Bangladesh) from 1970–2022, working in parishes and serving mostly in the education-formation apostolate of seminarians, religious, catechists, and lay leaders. He holds both licentiate and doctorate degrees in Missiology (Mission Theology) from the Gregorian University in Rome. His areas of specialization include Christology, Ecclesiology, Missiology, Vatican II, "Asian Theology" and the pontificate of Pope Francis. Contact data: jhkroeger@gmail.com.

Kroeger has produced numerous theological-missiological-catechetical books and articles, widely published throughout Asia. Orbis Books at Maryknoll has published *Walking with Pope Francis: The Official Documents in Everyday Language*; *The Gift of Mission: Yesterday, Today, Tomorrow*; *Once upon a Time in Asia: Stories of Harmony and Peace*; and *Living Mission: Challenges in Evangelization Today*.

Made in the USA
Monee, IL
23 April 2024

57363559R00036